Layers of Learning
Year One • Unit Two

Ancient Egypt
Map Keys
Stars
Ancient Egyptian Art

HooDoo Publishing
United States of America
©2014 Layers of Learning
Copies of maps or activities may be made for a particular family or classroom.
ISBN 978-1494289423

If you wish to reproduce or print excerpts of this publication, please contact us at contact@layers-of-learning.com for permission. Thank you for respecting copyright laws.

Units At A Glance: Topics For All Four Years of the Layers of Learning Program

1	History	Geography	Science	The Arts
1	Mesopotamia	Maps & Globes	Planets	Cave Paintings
2	Egypt	Map Keys	Stars	Egyptian Art
3	Europe	Global Grids	Earth & Moon	Crafts
4	Ancient Greece	Wonders	Satellites	Greek Art
5	Babylon	Mapping People	Humans in Space	Poetry
6	The Levant	Physical Earth	Laws of Motion	List Poems
7	Phoenicians	Oceans	Motion	Moral Stories
8	Assyrians	Deserts	Fluids	Rhythm
9	Persians	Arctic	Waves	Melody
10	Ancient China	Forests	Machines	Chinese Art
11	Early Japan	Mountains	States of Matter	Line & Shape
12	Arabia	Rivers & Lakes	Atoms	Color & Value
13	Ancient India	Grasslands	Elements	Texture & Form
14	Ancient Africa	Africa	Bonding	African Tales
15	First North Americans	North America	Salts	Creative Kids
16	Ancient South America	South America	Plants	South American Art
17	Celts	Europe	Flowering Plants	Jewelry
18	Roman Republic	Asia	Trees	Roman Art
19	Christianity	Australia & Oceania	Simple Plants	Instruments
20	Roman Empire	You Explore	Fungi	Composing Music

2	History	Geography	Science	The Arts
1	Byzantines	Turkey	Climate & Seasons	Byzantine Art
2	Barbarians	Ireland	Forecasting	Illumination
3	Islam	Arabian Peninsula	Clouds & Precipitation	Creative Kids
4	Vikings	Norway	Special Effects	Viking Art
5	Anglo Saxons	Britain	Wild Weather	King Arthur Tales
6	Charlemagne	France	Cells and DNA	Carolingian Art
7	Normans	Nigeria	Skeletons	Canterbury Tales
8	Feudal System	Germany	Muscles, Skin, & Cardiopulmonary	Gothic Art
9	Crusades	Balkans	Digestive & Senses	Religious Art
10	Burgundy, Venice, Spain	Switzerland	Nerves	Oil Paints
11	Wars of the Roses	Russia	Health	Minstrels & Plays
12	Eastern Europe	Hungary	Metals	Printmaking
13	African Kingdoms	Mali	Carbon Chem	Textiles
14	Asian Kingdoms	Southeast Asia	Non-metals	Vivid Language
15	Mongols	Caucasus	Gases	Fun With Poetry
16	Medieval China & Japan	China	Electricity	Asian Arts
17	Pacific Peoples	Micronesia	Circuits	Arts of the Islands
18	American Peoples	Canada	Technology	Indian Legends
19	The Renaissance	Italy	Magnetism	Renaissance Art I
20	Explorers	Caribbean Sea	Motors	Renaissance Art II

3	History	Geography	Science	The Arts
1	Age of Exploration	Argentina and Chile	Classification & Insects	Fairy Tales
2	The Ottoman Empire	Egypt and Libya	Reptiles & Amphibians	Poetry
3	Mogul Empire	Pakistan & Afghanistan	Fish	Mogul Arts
4	Reformation	Angola & Zambia	Birds	Reformation Art
5	Renaissance England	Tanzania & Kenya	Mammals & Primates	Shakespeare
6	Thirty Years' War	Spain	Sound	Baroque Music
7	The Dutch	Netherlands	Light & Optics	Baroque Art I
8	France	Indonesia	Bending Light	Baroque Art II
9	The Enlightenment	Korean Pen.	Color	Art Journaling
10	Russia & Prussia	Central Asia	History of Science	Watercolors
11	Conquistadors	Baltic States	Igneous Rocks	Creative Kids
12	Settlers	Peru & Bolivia	Sedimentary Rocks	Native American Art
13	13 Colonies	Central America	Metamorphic Rocks	Settler Sayings
14	Slave Trade	Brazil	Gems & Minerals	Colonial Art
15	The South Pacific	Australasia	Fossils	Principles of Art
16	The British in India	India	Chemical Reactions	Classical Music
17	Boston Tea Party	Japan	Reversible Reactions	Folk Music
18	Founding Fathers	Iran	Compounds & Solutions	Rococo
19	Declaring Independence	Samoa and Tonga	Oxidation & Reduction	Creative Crafts I
20	The American Revolution	South Africa	Acids & Bases	Creative Crafts II

4	History	Geography	Science	The Arts
1	American Government	USA	Heat & Temperature	Patriotic Music
2	Expanding Nation	Pacific States	Motors & Engines	Tall Tales
3	Industrial Revolution	U.S. Landscapes	Energy	Romantic Art I
4	Revolutions	Mountain West States	Energy Sources	Romantic Art II
5	Africa	U.S. Political Maps	Energy Conversion	Impressionism I
6	The West	Southwest States	Earth Structure	Impressionism II
7	Civil War	National Parks	Plate Tectonics	Post-Impressionism
8	World War I	Plains States	Earthquakes	Expressionism
9	Totalitarianism	U.S. Economics	Volcanoes	Abstract Art
10	Great Depression	Heartland States	Mountain Building	Kinds of Art
11	World War II	Symbols and Landmarks	Chemistry of Air & Water	War Art
12	Modern East Asia	The South States	Food Chemistry	Modern Art
13	India's Independence	People of America	Industry	Pop Art
14	Israel	Appalachian States	Chemistry of Farming	Modern Music
15	Cold War	U.S. Territories	Chemistry of Medicine	Free Verse
16	Vietnam War	Atlantic States	Food Chains	Photography
17	Latin America	New England States	Animal Groups	Latin American Art
18	Civil Rights	Home State Study	Instincts	Theater & Film
19	Technology	Home State Study II	Habitats	Architecture
20	Terrorism	America in Review	Conservation	Creative Kids

Unit 1-2 Printable Pack

This unit includes printables at the end. To make life easier for you we also created digital printable packs for each unit. To retrieve your printable pack for Unit 1-2, please visit

www.layers-of-learning.com/digital-printable-packs/

Put the printable pack in your shopping cart and use this coupon code:

1127UNIT1-2

Your printable pack will be free.

LAYERS OF LEARNING INTRODUCTION

This is part of a series of units in the Layers of Learning homeschool curriculum, including the subjects of history, geography, science, and the arts. Children from 1st through 12th can participate in the same curriculum at the same time - family school style.

The units are intended to be used in order as the basis of a complete curriculum (once you add in a systematic math, reading, and writing program). You begin with Year 1 Unit 1 no matter what ages your children are. Spend about 2 weeks on each unit. You pick and choose the activities within the unit that appeal to you and read the books from the book list that are available to you or find others on the same topic from your library. We highly recommend that you use the timeline in every history section as the backbone. Then flesh out your learning with reading and activities that highlight the topics you think are the most important.

Alternatively, you can use the units as activity ideas to supplement another curriculum in any order you wish. You can still use them with all ages of children at the same time.

When you've finished with Year One, move on to Year Two, Year Three, and Year Four. Then begin again with Year One and work your way through the years again. Now your children will be older, reading more involved books, and writing more in depth. When you have completed the sequence for the second time, you start again on it for the third and final time. If your student began with Layers of Learning in 1st grade and stayed with it all the way through she would go through the four year rotation three times, firmly cementing the information in her mind in ever increasing depth. At each level you should expect increasing amounts of outside reading and writing. High schoolers in particular should be reading extensively, and if possible, participating in discussion groups.

☺ ☺ ☺ These icons will guide you in spotting activities and books that are appropriate for the age of child you are working with. But if you think an activity is too juvenile or too difficult for your kids, adjust accordingly. The icons are not there as rules, just guides.

☺ GRADES 1-4
☺ GRADES 5-8
☺ GRADES 9-12

Within each unit we share:
- EXPLORATIONS, activities relating to the topic;
- EXPERIMENTS, usually associated with science topics;
- EXPEDITIONS, field trips;
- EXPLANATIONS, teacher helps or educational philosophies.

In the sidebars we also include Additional Layers, Famous Folks, Fabulous Facts, On the Web, and other extra related topics that can take you off on tangents, exploring the world and your interests with a bit more freedom. The curriculum will always be there to pull you back on track when you're ready.

You can learn more about how to use this curriculum at www.layers-of-learning.com/layers-of-learning-program/

ANCIENT EGYPT – MAP KEYS - STARS – ANCIENT EGYPTIAN ART

UNIT TWO
ANCIENT EGYPT – MAP KEYS – STARS – ANCIENT EGYPTIAN ART

The most beautiful thing we can experience is the mysterious. It is the source of all true art and all science. He to whom this emotion is a stranger, who can no longer pause to wonder and stand rapt in awe, is as good as dead: his eyes are closed.
- Albert Einstein

LIBRARY LIST:

HISTORY

Search for: Ancient Egypt, pyramids, mummies

😊 😊 😊 The Egyptian Cinderella by Shirley Climo. One of the world's oldest Cinderella stories.

😊 Bill and Pete by Tomie dePaola. The fictional story of a crocodile and his toothbrush, a plover (bird who eats bugs out of crocodiles' teeth), who live in the Nile. DePaola has written several picture books about Bill and Pete.

😊 Growing Up In Ancient Egypt by Rosalie David. Tells about life in ancient Egypt from a child's perspective.

😊 😊 Mummies In the Morning by Mary Pope Osborne. Look for the non-fiction companion book *Mummies and Pyramids*.

😊 😊 Into the Mummy's Tomb by Nicholas Reeves. A look at the discovery of King Tut's tomb.

😊 😊 Tutankhamen's Gift by Robert Sabuda. Tells the story of young King Tut restoring the worship of the many Egyptian gods and goddesses after his predecessor was monotheistic.

😊 😊 Secrets of the Mummies by Harriet Griffey. Find out how the Egyptians made mummies and read of the discovery of King Tut's tomb. Highly recommended.

😊 😊 Pharaoh's Boat by David Weitzman. Explains the construction and history and archeology of one special boat from Cheop's pyramid tomb.

😊 Mara, Daughter of the Nile by Eloise Jarvis McGraw. Novel for middle grades with a strong, but feminine female main character.

😊 Life in Ancient Egypt by John Green. A coloring book with detailed captions from Dover Publishers.

😊 😊 Eyewitness: Ancient Egypt by George Hart. A non-fiction overview of ancient Egypt.

😊 😊 Pyramid by David Macaulay. An inside look at the architecture and building methods of the most massive structures on earth. Amazing illustrations.

😊 😊 Cat of Bubastes by G.A. Henty. The sacred cat must be protected from assassins. Henty's novels center around young people undertaking exciting adventures using courage, ingenuity, and compassion.

😊 😊 The Golden Goblet by Eloise Jarvis McGraw. A young teen boy must guard the tombs against a gang of thieves.

Ancient Egypt – Map Keys - Stars – Ancient Egyptian Art

Geography

Search for: maps, keys
- If Maps Could Talk by Erika L. Shores. How to use map keys and symbols.
- Maps and Symbols by Susan Lomas.
- Map Scales by Mary Dodson Wade. Look for other "Read About Rookie" books on map topics.
- Maps and Mapping by Barbara Taylor. Information plus fun activities.
- Problem Solving With Maps by Stuart Marson. More challenging activities for older kids.
- Looking at Maps by Barbara Taylor.
- Be An Expert with Map and Compass by Bjorn Kjellstrom. Orienteering instruction guide for those serious about finding their way.

Science

Search for: stars, astronomy, constellations
- Find the Constellations by H.A. Rey. By far the best beginner constellation book. If you've never been able to see those elusive pictures in the night sky or pick out and identify one star, this book is for you.
- The Stars: A New Way to See Them by H.A. Rey. He knows how to teach neophytes about finding the stars.
- Glow-In-The-Dark Constellations by C.E. Thompson. A simple field guide to the constellations to take with you on a star gazing outing.
- Seeing in the Dark from PBS. Video of telescopes and the wonders of space.
- Starry Sky by Kate Hayden. An easy reader book from DK.
- Stars Beneath Your Bed by April Pulley Sayre. A picture book for young kids all about how the same dust that makes up the stars makes up us.
- Stars by Seymour Simon. Lots of information and beautiful pictures by one of the leading science authors for kids.
- Extreme Stars Q&A from the Smithsonian Institute.
- A Stargazer's Guide by Isaac Asimov.
- Bedroom Astronomy by the editors of Klutz. An engaging activity book covering physics of stars to constellations and their mythology.
- Black Holes, Pulsars, and Quasars by Isaac Asimov. A challenging book about advanced star concepts.
- The Life and Death of Stars by Isaac Asimov.
- Epitome of Copernican Astronomy by Johannes Kepler.

The Arts

Search for: ancient Egyptian art
- Ancient Egyptian Art by Susie Hodge. Tomb paintings and sculpture.
- The Art of Ancient Egypt by Gay Robins. Excellent overview for teens and adults.
- Ancient Egyptian Art—The Fun Way! By Florence Schatz. Explains the art in the context of the history and culture of ancient Egypt. Includes projects to try.
- The Encyclopedia of Ancient Egyptian Architecture by Dieter Arnold.

ANCIENT EGYPT – MAP KEYS – STARS – ANCIENT EGYPTIAN ART

HISTORY: ANCIENT EGYPT

Why was Upper Egypt to the south and Lower Eygpt to the north?

Well, because the Nile River which runs through it runs from the south to the north. Upper Egypt would have been upstream and lower Egypt was further downstream.

Fabulous Fact

The word "pharaoh" means great house. Originally it was the name for the king's palace, but eventually Egyptian rulers took it on as a title.

Joseph interpreting Pharaoh's dream by James Jacques Joseph Tissot.

Fabulous Fact

The Nile River is the longest river in the world. It begins in the south and flows north up to the Mediterranean Sea. Learn more about the Nile.

Like Mesopotamia, Egypt was another cradle of civilization. The Nile River provided enough water and very fertile farmland, making it possible for cities to grow up. Egyptian civilization flourished along the banks of the Nile. The people specialized into many kinds of jobs; there were farmers, stone carvers, scribes, priests, weavers, miners, merchants, embalmers, and potters. Egyptians developed two nations: Upper Egypt (to the south) and Lower Egypt (to the north). Eventually the two nations were combined through conquest into one. Later Egypt was taken over by a series of foreigners, the first being a tribe called the Hyksos.

The Nile River

The Egyptian kings were called pharaohs. The Egyptians considered their pharaohs to be gods. Cheops, Hatsheput, and Tutankhamen (sometimes called King Tut) were some of the best known pharaohs. The religion of ancient Egypt, like the religions of most people on earth, defined their everyday life. Temples and priests were central to their lives. Generations of people wore themselves out building huge monuments, the pyramids, to their pharaohs. The taxes collected supported the priests and the temples, as well as the army and rulers.

The pyramids are perhaps the things ancient Egyptians are best remembered for. The pyramids were tombs for pharaohs and other important people. Pharaohs were mummified and then buried in tombs filled with treasures and things for the pharaoh to use in the afterlife. The Pyramid of Khufu is the biggest of all the pyramids of Egypt and the only wonder of the Seven Wonders of the Ancient World that still stands today.

ANCIENT EGYPT – MAP KEYS - STARS – ANCIENT EGYPTIAN ART

☺ ☺ ☺ **EXPLORATION: Ancient Egyptian Map**
Use the map of ancient Egypt found at the end of this unit. Make a copy for each student.
- Color the Nile and the cataracts on the Nile.
- Label the Bahariya, Dakhla, and Kharga Oases, color.
- Draw trade route lines.
- Color code the Old, Middle, and New Kingdoms of Egypt; the later kingdoms included the territory of the old plus.
- Color the water blue and the deserts brown.
- Make a key and label the compass rose.

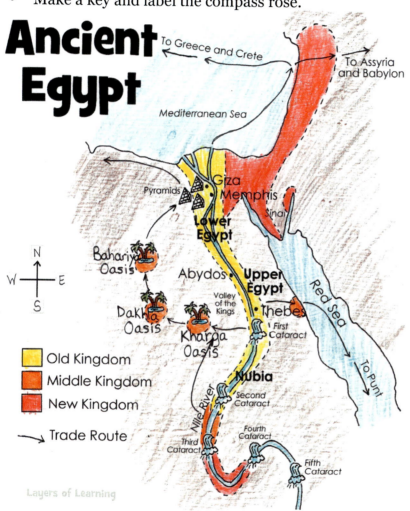

Fabulous Fact
Elephantine is an island in the middle of the Nile River near the First Cataract. (You may want to add it to your map of Egypt.) It is thought to be a sacred island and has a temple on it. Go find out more about this island, why it's called Elephantine, and its place in Egyptian myths.

Explanation
Kids really struggle with some subjects from time to time, whether it's learning to read or studying algebra. Sometimes the frustration and stress bring them to the brink and they become weepy or defiant or start to cheat. That's a good time to pour on a little more love.

One thing that invariably works with my boys is to set them on my lap. The close proximity, the physical touch, is reassuring and relaxing. An assignment that was too hard a minute ago suddenly becomes so easy just because they have loving arms around them.

Michelle

EXPLANATION: How To Utilize Timelines
Timelines are most useful for the middle grades and above (beginning no earlier than 3rd grade). Very young children don't have a well developed sense of time. Use a long paper from a roll; about 12-24 inches wide and 4-8 feet long is a good size. (Or you can tape pieces of paper together.) Draw a long line down the center of the timeline from left to right. Mark off the timeline into equal sections and label each mark with a year. Print out the

Ancient Egypt – Map Keys - Stars – Ancient Egyptian Art

Memorization Station

Principle Pharaohs of Egypt:

- Menes
- Zoser (Djoser)
- Khufu (Cheops)
- Mentuhotep
- Hyksos Kings in Lower Egypt
- Ahmose reunites Egypt
- Amenhotep I-III
- Thutmose I-IV
- Hatshepsut
- Akhenaten
- Tutenkhamen
- Ramses I-XI
- Sheshonq I
- Rule of Nubians
- Psammatichus I
- Rule of Persians
- Nectanebo
- Alexander the Great

Teaching Tip

All too often we focus on the wrong things in history lessons. Instead of worrying about memorizing facts, think of history as learning the stories of the people who have lived in our world. They probably weren't so different from us. Find parallels between the ancients and your family.

events along with a picture to represent them, or hand label and draw a picture to go with the event. Place each event along the timeline at the proper year and post the timeline up on the wall. Refer to it often as you learn about the civilization and try to make connections between the events you have posted.

Have your high schooler keep a comprehensive timeline of world history in a notebook. Use blank paper, draw a line down the center from left to right and date it. In the ancient times each page might be a century. As you get closer to modern times there will be much more information to fill in and you'll want the pages to cover fewer years.

If you like, write dates and events in with a color coded system to make it easier to find info you are looking for. You can do this two different ways, either coding according to a category, like science and technology, wars, rulers, arts, religion, etc. or you can code it according to civilization, all Egypt is written in red, Babylon is green, and so on.

☺ ☺ ☺ **EXPLORATION: Ancient Egyptian Timeline**
For Ancient Egypt, the timeline will cover from 5000 BC to 332 BC, a period of 4668 years, so you'll want to the mark the timeline in 500 year increments. Do the timeline early in your study, put it up on the wall and refer to it and add to it as you study ancient Egypt. We keep a timeline going for our whole year of study and add to it with each new unit. It becomes a centerpiece for our discussions and helps us keep track of what was happening in our world. At the end of this unit you will find timeline squares to print and place on a wall timeline or in a notebook timeline.

Here are some important dates to get you started:
- 5000 BC Farming starts in the Nile Valley
- 3100 BC King Menes unites Upper and Lower Egypt
- 3100 BC Hieroglyphic writing developed
- 2700-2500 BC Pyramids built

ANCIENT EGYPT – MAP KEYS - STARS – ANCIENT EGYPTIAN ART

- 2686 BC The Old Kingdom begins
- 2180 BC The Old Kingdom ends in famine and civil war
- 2040 BC Egypt is united again. The Middle Kingdom begins.
- 2040 BC Thebes becomes the capitol
- 1720 BC Egypt is invaded by the Hyksos, ending the Middle Kingdom
- 1550 BC New Kingdom period begins
- 1500 BC Valley of the Kings burials begin
- 1479 BC Reign of Pharaoh Hatshepsut, one of the few female pharaohs
- 1350 BC Amenhotep bans worship of Egyptian gods
- 1333 BC Reign of King Tut begins
- 1330 BC Tut restores old gods
- 1275 BC Ramses II defeats Hittites at Battle of Kadesh
- 1180 BC Ramses III defeats Sea Peoples
- 1070 BC Assyria makes Egypt a vassal nation
- 664 BC Last Egyptian Pharaoh falls to Persia
- 332 BC Alexander the Great conquers Egypt

☺ ☻ EXPLORATION: Gift of the Nile

Egypt is often called "the gift of the Nile." Can you guess how it got this name? Look at the land around Egypt; it's mostly desert that is hot and dry. Without the Nile River it is unlikely that a civilization of people ever would have grown up there, so indeed Egypt is the gift of the Nile. Every year the Nile floods for a few weeks. The ancient Egyptians were able to save the flood waters in canals and make it last the whole year. The floods made the soil nice and fertile so crops could be grown there.

Try this:
1. Put soil into a little baking dish – the bottom of the Nile.
2. Pour some water over the dirt – that's the flowing Nile River waters.
3. Next, put the little baking dish into a bigger baking dish – the big dish represents the dry desert.
4. Each spring when the snow melts off the mountains it all runs down and floods the Nile River. There's so much water during the floods that it overflows the Nile and water bursts right out of its banks! Pour water into the small baking dish until it overflows into the bigger one. The Egyptians could then

Writer's Workshop

Choose one of these Egyptian proverbs to illustrate and write neatly in your best handwriting.

Man fears time, but time fears the pyramids.

There is no darkness like ignorance.

Little is better than nothing.

One falsehood spoils a thousand truths.

The teeth are smiling, but is the heart?

Fabulous Fact

The Nile flooded every year between June and September. During the "off" season farmers were sent to work on one of the pharaoh's building projects.

The floods were said to be sent by Hapi, god of the Nile to bring fertility to the river valley.

Photo by Ian Sewell.

Ancient Egypt – Map Keys - Stars – Ancient Egyptian Art

Additional Layer
If you got an infection in ancient Egypt, you were prescribed to eat moldy bread. Today you might be given penicillin. How are they related?

Fabulous Fact
Natron, used to dry out mummies, is made of salts, about 17% of which is baking soda, or sodium bicarbonate.

Mummies By the Millions

Not only kings and royals were mummified in ancient Egypt, everybody was. Modern people found mummies by the millions, shipped them all over the world, displayed them, dissected them, held mummy unwrapping parties, and ground up mummy parts for use in tonics and medicines.

have nice, moist soil for growing crops, and also have leftover water to use to irrigate their crops when the soil began to dry out.

😊 😊 😊 EXPERIMENT: Fertile Soil
Because the Nile River provided fertile soil, the Egyptians were able to grow plenty of food for their people. Do a little test to see how crops grow in moist soil versus dry sand.

Gather sand, potting soil, a package of seeds (bean seeds work well), and 2 pots or jars. Put sand into one pot and potting soil into the other. Plant a bean seed in each one, and then chart its growth rate once a week for at least a month. You can give both seeds the same amount of water, or you could give the sand one (which represents the desert where there is little rain) half as much water as the soil filled pot. Before you begin, make a hypothesis. Then chart your progress and record your results.

😊 😊 EXPLORATION: Treasures and Tutankhamen
King Tutankhamen was a pharaoh who was famous for two simple reasons: (1) he was just a young boy — only 9 years old when he became the pharaoh and 18 when he died, and (2) his tomb was discovered almost untouched by grave robbers. One of the major drawbacks of having a huge pyramid as your final resting place was that tomb robbers could easily find the treasures you had hidden there. Almost all of the pyramids were robbed of their riches centuries ago. King Tut's tomb, in a hidden cave in the Valley of the Kings and not in a pyramid at all, had not been discovered until 1922, and was full of all sorts of treasures, including his throne, his golden bed, his ornate scarab, and his death mask. Pharaohs' tombs were also typically filled with the things they would need in the afterlife like food, money, and clothing.

If you could take things that were buried with you to a next life, what would you want in your tomb? Make a top ten list of ten things you own that you would want to take along after you died.

To learn a lot more about this topic, read *Secrets of the Mummies* from the library list in this unit.

😊 😊 EXPLORATION: Pharaoh Frank
Ancient Egyptians mummified important people like pharaohs and their wives to preserve their bodies for the afterlife. Here's what you need to mummify Pharaoh Frank:

- a hot dog

ANCIENT EGYPT – MAP KEYS - STARS – ANCIENT EGYPTIAN ART

- a plastic container that will fit a hot dog inside it
- baking soda
- a ruler
- a piece of floss, string, or yarn

Put several inches of baking soda inside your plastic container. Measure your hot dog, Pharaoh Frank, and write down how long he is. Measure his circumference by wrapping a string around him and measuring the string too. Write that down. You may also want to write down a few observations you make about what Pharaoh Frank looks like.

Now put him into the baking soda and add even more soda on top until he is covered with a few inches of baking soda. Let him sit for a bit. After 10 days, pull him out and start the process again. Take his measurements and write down your observations, then put him back in the container tomb with fresh, new baking soda. Leave him for another 10 days. Now your mummy should be ready! Pull him out and make your final measurements and observations.

What happened? Why do you think he looks like that? (The trick is water! The baking soda took all the water out of the hot dog to preserve it. It can't rot without any water in it, so your mummy, Pharaoh Frank, is now preserved for posterity.)

☺ ☻ EXPLORATION: Guardian Sphinx

The Great Sphinx is a statue of a man's head (thought to be Pharaoh Khufu of Egypt) on the head of a lion. It's the biggest monolith statue in the world. It sits near the pyramids at Giza as if to guard them. There are many myths and stories about sphinxes and their purposes, one of which is to be a guardian. If you needed a guardian for your house that was made of two (or more) different animals, which animals would you choose?

Draw a picture of your guardian and then write about why you

Fabulous Fact

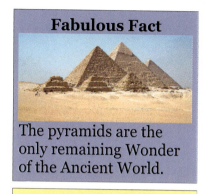

The pyramids are the only remaining Wonder of the Ancient World.

Explanation

A note about testing: There is a place for testing later on in academia, but developmentally speaking, this doesn't involve young children. Once a child reaches the formal operations stage of learning (able to think conceptually and in terms of abstract ideas) they should then be able to translate their concrete knowledge to a test answer sheet. Kids *should* learn to take tests. They *should* study for the SAT and ACT tests. They shouldn't leave for college or the job market without these essential skills. However, while kids are still gaining the bulk of their knowledge and learning to classify and connect, it is not the time. At least until they are teens, the focus should primarily be on learning to learn, not to take tests.

Ancient Egypt – Map Keys - Stars – Ancient Egyptian Art

Famous Folks

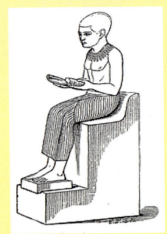

Imhotep was a scholar, architect, politician, engineer, poet, philosopher, artist, and physician to the great pharaoh, Djoser. His name means "one who comes in peace." He was deified at death and now stands next to the gods in importance.

Famous Folks

Hatshepshut (1494–1482 B.C.), Sobeknefru (1790–1782 B.C.), and Nitokris (2184–2181 B.C) were all female pharaohs of Egypt.

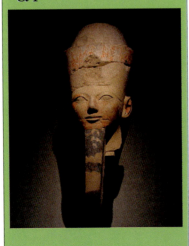

chose each animal on your picture. What animals did you choose to have guard you and what do they represent to you? What do we use to guard us modernly?

☺ ☻ ☻ EXPLORATION: Mystery of the Missing Nose

The nose on the Great Sphinx is missing, but no one knows what happened to it for sure.

Some believe that Muhammed Sa'im al-Dahr destroyed it in an attempt to fight the Egyptian religion when he saw peasants making offerings to it to increase their harvest. Some people believe that a cannonball shot from one of Napoleon's armies blasted the nose off. Use your imagination to create a story of what you think may have happened to the Sphinx's nose.

☺ ☻ ☻ EXPLORATION: Death Mask

The mummies of pharaohs had death masks placed over their heads. The mask was an idealized image of how the pharaoh would look in the afterlife. Create your own death mask using a milk jug, 3 paper plates, some paper maché, and paints.

Start by cutting your milk jug. Cut it in half along the seam beginning with the neck of the jug. Save the side with the handle. Cut the bottom off along the seam as well. Next, cut the paper plates in half and staple them together on to your milk jug.

Ancient Egypt – Map Keys - Stars – Ancient Egyptian Art

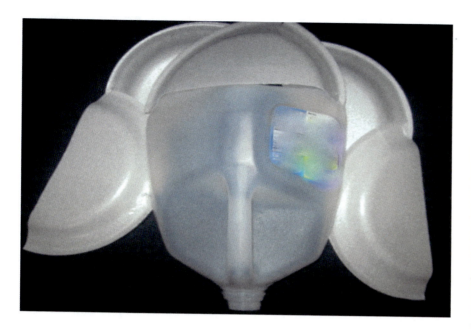

Propaganda For the Ages

Ramses II suffered a defeat against the Hittites at Kadesh in 1288 B.C.

He erected a monument of victory anyway, extolling his prowess as a military leader. Everybody believed in the victory of Ramses until recent archaeologists dug up the truth.

Now take strips of newspaper and dip them into a flour and water paper maché paste (2 cups hot water to 1 cup flour), then layer them onto the mask form. Keep layering until the whole mask is completely covered, and then let it dry thoroughly. (Can take several days or up to a week.)

Cleopatra's Needle

Two obelisks were built in ancient Egypt as markers and monuments.

Now there's one in New York and another in London. Neither actually have any connection with Cleopatra, as they were made long before she was born. Still, the name sounds nice.

Finally, paint your mask. You may want to include some gold paint because it was traditional for death masks to look very rich!

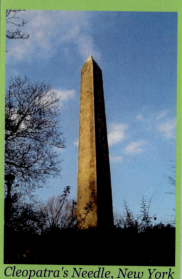

Cleopatra's Needle, New York City.

Ancient Egypt – Map Keys – Stars – Ancient Egyptian Art

Memorization Station

Here is a poem written by an anonymous Egyptian about his country:

*Its fields are full of good things and it has provision for every day
Its granaries overflow, they reach the sky.
Its ponds are full of fishes and its lakes of birds.
Its fields are green with grass and its banks bear dates.
He who lives there is happy,
And the poor man is like the great elsewhere.*

Additional Layer

Look up the amazing story of Cleopatra and the asp to see how it changed Egypt forever.

Famous Folks

Pepi II of Egypt (2294 to 2220 B.C.) reigned for 74 years. He kept slaves nearby who were smothered in honey, so the flies would be attracted to them.

You'll also find a coloring page of King Tut's Death Mask in the printables section.

😊 😊 EXPLORATION: Scarab Seal

Egyptians put their wax or clay seals onto important documents to seal them (kind of like how we lick envelopes and write our return address on them before putting them in the mail.) Seals were often made to look like a scarab, a beetle that symbolized the sun and was honored by Egyptians. Mold a clay scarab, carve details to make it look like a beetle on top, and put your initials (or a picture that represents you) on to the bottom of it. Let it dry completely or bake it to dry it out. Then use your scarab seal and an ink pad to stamp the seal on to a letter and envelope.

😊 😊 EXPLORATION: Adorned Egyptians

Appearance was very important to Egyptians, especially the wealthy and powerful ones. The men and women wore wigs, make-up, and jewelry. Make some of your own jewelry. Start by gathering a few supplies:

- a toilet paper roll
- scissors
- paints and brushes
- sequins or other decor (optional)

ANCIENT EGYPT – MAP KEYS – STARS – ANCIENT EGYPTIAN ART

To make wrist bangles, cut a toilet paper roll in half, then cut each half lengthwise. Paint them. Add sequin jewels or other decor. Now slip one on to each wrist for Egyptian style bracelets.

  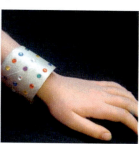

😊 😊 😊 EXPLORATION: Pyramid Report

Use the information you're learning about Egypt to write an informational report on pyramids. Begin by doing a bit of research and finding the answers to these questions:

- What are pyramids?
- What do they look like?
- How were they built?
- Who built the pyramids?
- Why were they built?
- When and where were pyramids built? Only in Egypt?
- Why are pyramids important?

Once you've answered these questions put them into a five paragraph report. You may want to use the sandwich report organizer from http://www.layers-of-learning.com/teaching-kids-to-write-their-first-reports/ to help you organize your information.

Younger kids will enjoy making a pyramid shaped report of four or five pages, one sentence per page.

Fabulous Fact

The largest pyramid in the world is Cholula in Mexico. It's a lot shorter than Cheops' pyramid but covers much more ground.

A Love Poem from Ancient Egypt

I hear thy voice, O turtle dove-
The dawn is all aglow-
Weary am I with love, with love,
Oh, whither shall I go?

Not so, O beauteous bird above,
Is joy to be denied....
For I have found my dear, my love;
And I am by his side.

We wander forth, and hand in hand
Through flowery ways we go-
I am the fairest in the land,
For he has called me so.

Additional Layer

Visit www.pbs.org and search for "scaling the pyramids" for a great geometry lesson that demonstrates just how big the pyramids really are.

Ancient Egypt – Map Keys – Stars – Ancient Egyptian Art

Fabulous Facts

The Great Pyramid is aligned exactly to true north, an amazing feat of engineering.

There are over 100 pyramids in Egypt that have been found so far. Many of them were buried in the sand for thousands of years before being re-discovered.

T To build a pyramid you needed a large population from which to take a workforce, lots of slaves gained in battle, a plentiful food supply, a great deal of wealth and power, and a stable government. Egypt achieved these things during the Old Kingdom period.

Some people say slaves built the pyramids, others that hired workers of Egypt did (perhaps as a tax?); or maybe it was both slaves and Egyptians? What do you think?

☺ ☺ ☺ EXPLORATION: Cartouch

The Egyptians had a different language and form of writing from the Mesopotamian people. They had two different ways to write: Coptic and hieroglyphic. The hieroglyphic was the writing of nobility and priests and the Coptic language was the everyday writing of the people. Eventually both languages were lost to

	a		b		d		e/i		f/v		g
	h		j		c/k		l		m		n
	o/u		p		q		r		s		t
	w		x		y		z				

time, but found once more and translated in modern times by scholars. The civilizations about whom we know the most were those who kept written records which we can now read. The people of northern Europe kept no written record that we have found, and so we know very little about them. The people of the Indus Valley kept many records, but we cannot read them, and so we know very little about them. Because we can read the writings of the ancient Egyptians, we know a great deal about them.

Among the hieroglyphic writings found on the walls of tombs and the sides of temples are special figures known as cartouches. A cartouch is a name. The cartouch would be surrounded by an oval to set it apart from the rest of the symbols.

You can make a cartouch of your own.
1. Cut cardboard, such as from a cereal box, into an oval, about 5 inches long and 3 inches wide.
1. Spray paint it in a metallic paint to make it look fancy.
2. Then cut an oval from white or off-white paper just a bit smaller than the cardboard piece you already have.
3. Write your name in hieroglyphics on the paper.
4. Glue the paper to the cardboard. Decorate with sequins or glitter.
5. Hole punch the top and string a bit of ribbon through to hold it.

☺ ☺ ☺ EXPLORATION: Rosetta Stone

The Rosetta Stone was the key that allowed us to understand the writing of the ancient Egyptians. It had a decree that was written in 3 versions: hieroglyphics, Egyptian, and also Greek. Because the same thing was written in 3 ways scholars were able to decipher what the hieroglyphic symbols meant.

ANCIENT EGYPT – MAP KEYS - STARS – ANCIENT EGYPTIAN ART

Use a pie pan and some plaster of Paris to create your own Rosetta Stone. Go visit:http://www.quizland.com/hiero.htm.

It's an online hieroglyphics translator. Type whatever you'd like your stone to say and it will show you the hieroglyphic version of it. Mix up your plaster and pour it into the pie tin. Before it dries, use a skewer, toothpick, or sharp pencil to write your message in English and in hieroglyphics. You may want to write it in a 3rd language too. There are lots of online translators for any language you choose.

☺ ● EXPLORATION: Pyramid Model

There are well over 100 pyramids that have been discovered in Egypt alone. Most of them were built as tombs for Pharaohs. There is a lot of symbolism in the way they were built. For example, almost all Egyptian pyramids were built on the west bank of the Nile River, the side with the setting sun, which represents the mythological realm of the dead.

Use sugar cubes as building blocks and create your own pyramid. For mortar to hold the bricks together, combine 1 egg white with 1 1/2 cups powdered sugar and a pinch of cream of tartar. Beat it together until well combined. Using the mortar, glue together 10 rows of 10 sugar cubes each. Glue the rows together to form the square base of the pyramid. The next layer will be made with 9 rows of 9, then the next with 8 rows of 8, and so on until you have a single cube at the top.

☺ ☺ ● EXPLORATION: An Egyptian Creation Story

Here is the Egyptian story of how the world began.

The world began as a dark chaos of water called Nun. Out of the water rose a hill called Ben-Ben. On the hill stood Atum, the

Explanation

I like learning to be for the sake of learning as often as possible.

Instead of taking a weekly test, we play a weekly game show, kind of like *Are You Smarter Than A Fifth Grader*. I ask questions and anyone who knows the answer pops their hand up.

The questions can be anything we've learned about EVER. They encompass all subjects, and even cover things that weren't officially "school" topics. I jot down questions on index cards that sit on my desk. I keep all the questions we've ever used and they stay in the game, so eventually there are repeats. If no one answers the question right I try to put it towards the top where we'll hit it again really soon.

Our game show makes for a great review, and gives me a quick look at where the kids are, what they are remembering, and what we should probably go over again.

Ancient Egypt – Map Keys – Stars – Ancient Egyptian Art

Additional Layer

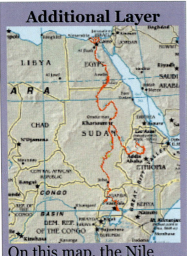

On this map, the Nile River is shown in red. Does that mean the river is actually red? Of course not— except for that one episode in the Bible. Colors on a map are used as symbols. And just like the Nile isn't really red, neither is the Red Sea really blue.

Additional Layer

The Nile River is fascinating to learn more about. It begins at Lake Victoria, the largest lake in Africa. One section of the river, the Sudd, is the world's biggest swamp. Grasses and reeds grow so thickly that they form floating islands tough enough for an elephant to stand on! The river runs different colors, and is named for them. The White Nile is a faster running whitewater portion, while the Blue Nile actually looks more blue.

first god. When Atum coughed, out came the god of air, Shu, and the goddess of moisture, Tefnut. Shu and Tefnut had children; Geb, the god of earth and Nut, the goddess of sky. Nut was lifted up to form a canopy over Geb. Then Nut and Geb had four children, Osiris, Isis, Seth, and Nephthys. Osiris and Isis ruled the earth until Seth became jealous and killed Osiris. Osiris became the god of the underworld and still welcomes all the dead into the next life. Seth became king of the world, but not for long. Osiris and Isis had a son named Horus. Horus battled with and defeated Seth and Horus became the king of the world, banishing Seth forever.

Make the story into a story book, one or two sentences on each page. You can copy the words from the story above or you can rephrase it in your own words. Illustrate each page. Each of the Egyptian gods and goddesses had definite physical features so look up what they looked like if you want to be authentic.

☺ ☻ EXPLORATION: Ozymandias

Read (and memorize if you wish) this poem by Percy Bysshe Shelley about an Egyptian King named Ramses, also translated as Ozymandias.

Ozymandias

I met a traveler from an antique land
Who said: Two vast and trunkless legs of stone
Stand in the desert. Near them on the sand,
Half sunk, a shatter'd visage lies, whose frown
And wrinkled lip and sneer of cold command
Tell that its sculptor well those passions read
Which yet survive, stamp'd on these lifeless things,
The hand that mock'd them and the heart that fed them.
And on the pedestal these words appear:
"My name is Ozymandias, king of kings:
Look on my works, ye mighty, and despair!"
Nothing beside remains. Round the decay
Of that colossal wreck, boundless and bare,
The lone and level sands stretch far away.

Discussion questions:
- What did the king want people to look at?
- What kinds of "works" did the Egyptians do?
- What was left in the sand near the statue?
- What message do you think the poem is trying to give?
- Do you agree with the ideas behind the poem?

ANCIENT EGYPT – MAP KEYS - STARS – ANCIENT EGYPTIAN ART

Geography: Map Reading

Maps are only useful if they can be read. Generally there isn't enough space on a map to actually write out the names and descriptions of each place the mapmaker wants to depict, so instead mapmakers use symbols. To help people read the map, they create a key. Besides the symbols, a map must tell the size of space the map is depicting. We call this the scale. Another big aspect of map reading is the compass rose. Most maps have north at the top of the map by convention, but they don't have to. A map can be oriented any way the map maker chooses. But it's impossible to read unless you can align the map with the real physical world.

Kids need lots of practice with these concepts when they are new, so they will be worked on continually over several years as you create and color maps from all the history and geography units coming up.

The three major concepts covered in this unit are:

- Keys & Symbols
- Scale
- Compass Rose

☺ ☺ ☺ **EXPLORATION: Scavenger Hunt**
Find the key on a map. Point out the symbols and what they mean. Find some of them on the map. Then do a scavenger hunt. Pick a symbol and tell the kids to find a city with a population of more than 100,000, or find a national park, or find a school. You can customize it to the map you have. Give the kids ten to twenty things to find, depending on how old they are.

☺ ☺ **EXPLORATION: Cut and Paste Map Key**
Make your own map with a key. Make copies of the city map from the end of this unit. Draw in your own symbols for the key, fill in the rectangles at the bottom of the map page with your symbols. Cut out your newly colored rectangles and place them on the map. Don't forget to fill in the compass rose.

You can also use this worksheet to teach your kids to follow directions, as in "do as you are told" and also cardinal directions. For example, you might tell them to place the fire station on the northwest corner of Arcturus Road and Ursa Major Way.

Map Vocab
Neatline: border of a map

Orientation: direction a map should face

Legend: clue to what the symbols on a map mean, same as the key.

Fabulous Fact
A map's title is very important and gives clues or direction as to how a map should be used. For example "Road Map of Washington State" is very different from "Population Distribution in Asia."

On The Web
http://www.mywonderfulworld.org/toolsforadventure/games/adventure.html

A great spot to learn about map keys in a game.

Additional Layer
Read about early navigators in the days before GPS. How did they find their way? What instruments did they use?

Ancient Egypt – Map Keys – Stars – Ancient Egyptian Art

Jobs where map reading is very important
Truck Driver
Soldier and Sailor
Mail / Package Delivery
Mom or Dad
Meter Reader
Realtor
Land Planner
Forester/ Land Manager
Emergency Dispatcher
Civil Engineer
Sales Representative
Police Officer
Fire Officer
Gas/Power Engineers
Installation Technician
Construction sub-contractor
Courier
Taxi Driver
Paramedic
Geographer

Maps Lie
All maps are less than completely accurate. They leave out information out of necessity, but more than that, people can use maps to purposely distort the truth.

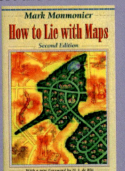

Learn more by reading *How To Lie With Maps* by Mark Monmonier, high school and up.

☺ ☻ EXPLORATION: Treasure Island Map
Copy the island map activity worksheet from the end of this unit. There's a fill-in-the-blank title so your kids can name their own island. Color the symbols in the key, then put each of the symbols on the map at least once. You can include more symbols as well if you like. Don't forget to label the compass rose.

Have the kids write directions to go with their map so that the treasure can be found.

☺ ☺ ☻ EXPLORATION: Map Scales
There are three ways map makers show scale. Sometimes a map will have more than one of these. They are:
- verbal method
- graphic method
- fractional method

The verbal method would be like this:

1 inch represents 1 mile

The graphic method is a picture:

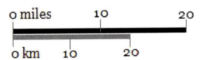

And the fractional method is like this:

1: 1,000,000

This means that one unit on the map equals 1,000,000 units on the ground.

Get some maps or an atlas and find these methods for scale. Measure the actual distances between two places using the map scales.

Then draw your own imaginary map and give it a scale.

☺ ☺ ☻ EXPLORATION: How Far?
Using a map of the world, find out how far it is from New York to London. Find the scale on the map. Use a scrap piece of paper and mark the length of the scale on the paper. Then see how many lengths it takes to get from New York to London. Multiply

Ancient Egypt – Map Keys – Stars – Ancient Egyptian Art

(or add) the number of lengths times the distance shown on the scale. Try it with several different city combinations.

😊 😊 😊 EXPLORATION: Imaginary World Tour

Using a world map, choose a city to start your imaginary world tour from. You're going to write a 10 page travelogue of a tour of 3 cities around the world. On each page you will need to draw a picture of the place and also write a description of your trip, where you are, and what you are doing. Here's the outline for your travelogue pages:

<u>Page 1:</u> Your city of origin. (You could draw yourself at home with bags packed, or a familiar landmark from your city.)
<u>Page 2:</u> Your first leg of travel. Are you going on a train? A plane? On a ship? How are you getting there? Don't forget to include how far you're going (you'll have to use your map scale to determine this).
<u>Page 3:</u> Your first destination. New York? Paris? Moscow? Cairo? Sydney? Dublin? Include a bit about what you get to see and do at your destination.
<u>Page 4:</u> Your second leg of travel... Will you go by car? Ride the subway? Hop on a bicycle? Include the distance you're traveling.
<u>Page 5:</u> Your second destination. Hong Kong? Orlando? Caracas? What was your favorite part?
<u>Page 6:</u> Your 3rd leg of travel... Will you take a bus? Windsurf? Go by helicopter?
<u>Page 7:</u> Your 3rd destination. Kabul? Abu Dhabi? Timbuktu? Where do you dream of going, and just what would you do there?
<u>Page 8:</u> Your 4th leg of travel. It's time for your trip to come to an end. How far away is home? How will you get there? By jet ski? In a tank? Aboard a submarine? How far was this leg?
<u>Page 9:</u> You...home again at last.
<u>Page 10</u>: Add up your mileage and tell how far you went all together.

😊 😊 EXPLORATION: English vs. Metric

Find the scale on several different maps. Are the scales the same on each map or different? Do all maps use the same units? Some may use feet or miles (which is typically used in America) while others use meters and kilometers (typically used throughout most other parts of the world). Some scales may show both.

😊 😊 EXPLORATION: My Bedroom

Make a scale map of your bedroom. Measure the floor space from wall to wall first. Now use graph paper and decide on your scale. You could have 1 square equal 1 foot or 1 square equal 2 feet, depending on how large you want your map (or use meters

Additional Layer

The mathematical principle used to make map scales is proportion. If maps weren't made proportionally to the distances of the real places they represent, they would be completely useless in determining distances.

Figure out the proportions of the map you made of your bedroom. Every 1 unit on your map represents how many units in real life?

Additional Layer

We now rely heavily on GPS (global positioning systems) more than we do on compasses. A compass uses magnetic fields. What does GPS use? Should we throw away our compasses now that we have GPS, or are there still some benefits to the tried-and-true map and compass methods of navigating? What limits are there to GPS? What limits are there to a compass?

Ancient Egypt – Map Keys - Stars – Ancient Egyptian Art

A compass rose can be a work of art

By Brosen and shared on Wikimedia commons

instead of feet). Now measure and plot your furniture and so on. Be sure to put a scale and compass rose on your bedroom map.

🙂 🙂 EXPLORATION: Compass Rose
Look at several maps and find the compass rose. Some are simple while others become works of art all by themselves. Design a compass rose. Include the cardinal directions: N, S, E, W; and the intermediate directions: NE, NW, SE, SW. Now add some details to make yours a work of art.

EXPLANATION: WE
North and south tend to be easy for kids to remember, but they often get the east and west mixed up when they are labeling a compass rose. It helps if you remember that they spell "WE." (They can also remember that when the sun rises, it's from east to west using the opposite: "EW" – say this like you're seeing a disgusting bug of course!)

🙂 🙂 🙂 EXPLORATION: Needle Compass
Make a simple compass. You need a bar magnet, needle, and shallow dish of water. Stroke the needle along the magnet in the same direction about 20 times. This will magnetize the needle. Then very carefully place the needle on the water to make it float. The magnetized needle will swing around and point north.

🙂 🙂 EXPLORATION: Orienteering Treasure Hunt
Orienteering just means finding your way with a map and

ANCIENT EGYPT – MAP KEYS - STARS – ANCIENT EGYPTIAN ART

compass. Set up a simple course in the backyard or a nearby park. First, show the kids how a compass has numbers all around the edges. Those numbers are degrees and they're the same as the degrees around a circle when they're doing math. So if I say, "Walk 10 degrees north," then you point the compass so north is lined up with the needle and then face your body toward the ten degree mark and walk ten paces.

Here's how you might set up a course: Have the kids take at least five or six compass bearings and have them walk so many paces between each compass mark. You may want to put out flags or markers at each location along the way to keep beginners on track, but don't make them so obvious that they don't need to use the compass at all. You'll have to go out ahead of time and run through it yourself, making sure you end up in a convenient location to hide a treat for your treasure hunters at the end.

☺ ☺ EXPLORATION: Triangle Course
Go to a park or open field area. Each participant needs to poke a pencil or stick into the ground at their starting location to mark it. Line up with north on your compass and choose a landmark (a tree, phone pole, etc.) off in the distance. Go 100 paces towards it, then stop. Next, set your compass to 120 degrees and go another 100 paces in that direction. Finally, set your compass to 240 degrees and pace your final 100 steps. You should have walked in a triangle and ended up at your starting point. Make it a game and see who can get closest to their starting marker.

☺ EXPEDITION: Real Orienteering
This is a challenging activity and best if one adult already knows how to do orienteering. Obtain a forest service topographical map for a wilderness area near you. Take a compass, the map, water, and other safety gear, and go on a hike where you must use a map and compass to find your way. For a simpler activity, hike a well established trail and have the kids note their new direction every time the trail makes a turn.

EXPLANATION: Learning Directions
From here on out kids should be drawing a compass rose on every map you complete for history or geography. You should also practice cardinal directions by talking about them as you drive around town: *"Now we're turning west . . . which way are we turning now?"* This will not only be helpful in their map studies, but also as they are learning practical directions and how to get around without getting lost.

Additional Layer

The compass was invented in China and used for navigation. What else was invented in China?

Additional Layer

Read *Carry On Mr. Bowditch* by Jean Latham. It's a story of a great American navigator for about fourth grade and up.

Writer's Workshop

Imagine you are lost and stranded in the wilderness. Write about how you will get back. Before you start writing decide on your setting, characters (this could include animals you encounter), and basic storyline. Mapping your basic storyline could include determining how you got into your predicament, what challenges you will encounter along the way, and how you will finally solve the problem. Now craft a catchy opening sentence and see where it takes you. . .*"The sun was just coming up over the mountains when the ground started to rumble. . . shake. . . crack. . . I barely escaped . . .*

ANCIENT EGYPT – MAP KEYS - STARS – ANCIENT EGYPTIAN ART

SCIENCE: STARS

Fabulous Fact

Today there are 88 recognized constellations.

Canis major and lepus painted by Sidney Hall (1825)

Fabulous Fact

The pole star, the star directly over the north pole, shifts over time as the earth wobbles on its axis.

In 3000 BC the star Thuban in the Draco constellation was the pole star, and in 3000 AD Gamma Cephei will be the pole star.

Additional Layer

Shooting stars aren't stars at all. They are actually meteoroids that appear to streak as they strike the atmosphere of the earth and get burned up.

Go find out the difference between a meteoroid and a meteorite.

The trillions of stars in the sky have been fascinating people throughout time. They are huge objects in space that give off light and heat. They go through changes, which we call the life cycle of the star. They begin as huge clouds made mostly of hydrogen gas. The hydrogen heats up as gravity pulls the cloud into a dense ball. As the hydrogen gets hotter and hotter it changes into a gas called helium, and a star is born. The energy made from the whole process is what is released as light and heat in space — that's what makes the glowing specks we see in the night sky. That's just the beginning of a star's life cycle though. Over billions of years the core, or center, of the star gets smaller and the outer layers start to move away. As it gets bigger, it also gets cooler. We call a star at this stage a red giant. As the outer layers drift away, the star becomes a white dwarf that is darkening and getting cooler and cooler all the time. This is the last part of a star's life cycle. Not all stars become white dwarf stars though; some explode instead! A star that has exploded is called a supernova.

Nebula, where stars are formed. Photo taken by the Hubble Space Telescope.

Not all stars are the same; they come in different sizes and different intensities. The size and intensity are due to the mass of the star and the age of the star, as well as the chemicals that make up the star. Here's a list of stars from largest and hottest to smallest and coolest (in general):

Ancient Egypt – Map Keys - Stars – Ancient Egyptian Art

- blue giant
- blue-white
- yellow-white
- yellow
- orange
- red dwarf
- brown or dark stars

Like people, stars don't all fit perfectly into categories. The sun is a medium-sized yellow star. Astronomers have recently discovered brown, or dark, stars. Like their name suggests, they are dark and can't be seen from Earth at all. So how do scientists know dark stars exist? Astronomy relies heavily on complex mathematical calculations of tiny (as seen from earth) variations in the way bodies in the universe move. When visible stars or planets move from their regular path we know they are responding to the gravity of another nearby body. Astronomers also notice when light changes in intensity, varies in color, or is bent. All these things give clues to things out there in the universe that we can't see at all.

Pleiades Cluster

But there are plenty of things we can see, even things we can see with the naked eye, the things the ancients could see as well. Much of the universe is mysterious to us even today. The ancients made up stories about the things they saw in the night sky. People are still making up stories about outer space and what might be out there. One of our favorite modern stories is the *Star Trek* series of TV shows, but the old stories are still very interesting as well. We call those stories "myths," and we still know about the ones told by the Greeks, Romans, Chinese, Arabs,

Memorization Station

Here are a few constellations to look for and remember in the northern hemisphere:

Spring:
- Leo (and the star Regulus)

Summer:
- The Big Dipper and Ursa Major
- The Little Dipper and Ursa Minor
- Polaris, the North Star
- The Dragon
- Cygnus (and the Northern Cross, plus the stars Deneb and Vega)

Winter:
- Taurus (and the Pleiades Cluster)
- Orion

This is Orion. The red star near the top is Betelgeuse.

Additional Layer

Stars are made of a type of matter called plasma. It's super excited gases that are zooming around like mad. If you are lucky you can see plasma in the northern lights.

Ancient Egypt – Map Keys – Stars – Ancient Egyptian Art

Additional Layer

Stars are burning on fusion power. They are combining two atoms into one. In the case of stars, it is hydrogen atoms (the very smallest and a very reactive type of atom) being combined to form helium, a stable noble gas. That process creates lots of heat and light.

Scientists on Earth have sort of achieved this type of reaction, but they're not very good at it and can't really control it. There will be a Nobel Prize for the one who does.

Fabulous Facts

Stars create stellar winds made of gases let off into space.

Astrophysicists are almost certain that black holes exist, but since we can't actually see them, we may be mistaken.

Stars twinkle because the atmosphere around earth bends and distorts the light.

Most of the stuff in stars is hydrogen and helium, but traces of all the elements are found in them.

and American Indians, among others. Most of these stories were told about patterns or pictures the ancient people thought they could see in the stars as they studied the night sky. We call these star pictures constellations.

Throughout history, stars have been used for navigation, orientation, for religious practices, and to create calendars. The oldest star chart ever found was made in ancient Egypt.

It's still useful today to get to know the constellations. Modern people most often learn the constellations the Greeks first described. Learning the constellations will help you become familiar with the night sky. It's really cool to look up there at thousands of stars and be able to quite casually remark to your friend, "Cygnus is looking particularly beautiful tonight."

☺ ☻ EXPLORATION: Star Classification

Stars are categorized according to the light they give off. The light is determined by their temperature and the chemical elements they are made of. The chart below show stars from coolest (T) to hottest (O).

Our sun is a class G star. The Pleiades Cluster is filled with blue class B stars. Vega is a bright class A star. Betelgeuse in the constellation Orion is a class M red super giant, one of the largest stars known.

Go outside on a clear night with a star chart or guide and find these stars mentioned above. Sometimes the star's color is very difficult to distinguish from Earth, mostly because of our atmosphere. Make a drawing showing several stars you find and their color.

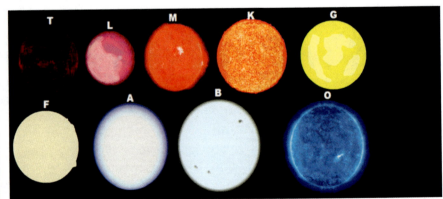

Image by Isna Kasamee and shared on Wikimedia Commons

This topic gets a whole lot deeper. Your older students may want to research more about star classification and phases online and in books from the library.

28

Ancient Egypt – Map Keys - Stars – Ancient Egyptian Art

😊 😊 EXPLORATION: Constellation Viewer

Make a pop can peep hole constellation viewer. Use an empty aluminum soda pop can. On a small piece of graph paper (small round to match the size of the bottom of the pop can) draw the stars of a constellation using a constellation guide book to help you. Once you have the stars plotted, flip the paper over and mark the stars from the reverse side. It is the reverse side you want facing out so that when you look at your constellation from inside of your can it will be facing the right way. Tape the graph paper to the bottom of the can and drive small nails through the paper and through the can at each "star" point. Look through the opening at your constellation. Cover the outside of the can with construction paper, decorated with the name of your constellation.

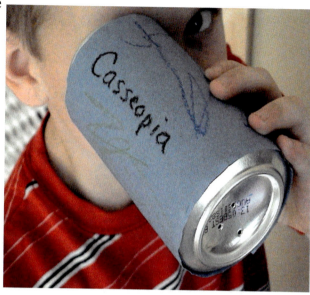

😊 😊 EXPLORATION: My Own Night Sky

Use glow-in-the-dark star stickers or glow-in-the-dark paint to put constellations on your ceiling. Pick a few of your favorites, place them carefully on your ceiling, then place extra stars around them. For a more accurate night sky on your ceiling purchase a child's constellation projector and paint a "star" in every place a lighted dot is projected on to your ceiling.

😊 😊 😊 EXPEDITION: Stargazing

This is one you'll want to repeat several times, or more likely from time to time throughout your life. Take a moonless evening and go some place dark out in the country. Bring a constellation guide book with you and try to spot several of the constellations and identify a few stars. Bring snacks, blankets, chairs and binoculars. There are star gazing clubs all over the country, and if you're interested you can join with them. That way you'll have some expert advice in helping you find the constellations. Otherwise, bring along a guidebook. Our favorite is *Find the Constellations* by H.A. Rey. There are also free smart phone apps that will help you find the stars and constellations using GPS.

Famous Folks

Probably the most famous modern astronomer is Steven Hawking of Britain. He's actually much more than a mere astronomer, he's a brilliant mathematician and astrophysicist. He wrote several popular books on astronomy and his name became well-known.

It's A Funny!

"There are 10^{11} stars in the universe. That used to be a *huge* number. But it's only a hundred billion. It's less than the national deficit! We used to call them astronomical numbers. Now we should call them economical numbers."

-Physicist Richard Feynman, 1987

Ancient Egypt – Map Keys – Stars – Ancient Egyptian Art

Additional Layer

Vincent Van Gogh was a famous painter who painted a very unique night sky called "Starry Night." Create your own starry painting.

😊 😊 😊 EXPEDITION: Armchair Astronomer

This is an armchair expedition you can take from the comfort of your home. Go on a tour of deep space by exploring the images from NASA at www.nasaimages.org or visit www.hubblesite.org. You'll be amazed.

EXPLANATION: Space Weather

Sign up online with Space Weather (www.spaceweather.com). They'll send you free e-mails about events in the heavens. You'll know when the International Space Station is flying overhead, when a particularly good aurora is expected, when to expect meteor showers, if a comet recently flew into the sun, and so on. For most astronomical events they'll send you a link in your e-mail to view the event as seen from observatories or amateur photographs and videos. Extremely cool.

😊 😊 😊 EXPLORATION: Life Cycle Of A Star

Just like people, stars are born, they live, and then they die. We can watch and photograph their life cycles. We know they form from nebulae of gases. A protostar, or new star, forms in the center of the cloud. The new star gives off light and heat. Over time the outside layers of the star move outward from the center. As they do, they begin to cool. The cooler layers on the outside start to drift off into space. Eventually, the star continues to get darker and cooler over time.

Copy off The Life Cycle of a Star worksheet from the end of this unit, one for each student. After learning about the life cycle of a star, complete the Life Cycle worksheet by labeling and coloring each stage.

Additional Layer

Explain how the earth rotates and makes it appear as though the stars and sun are moving through the sky.

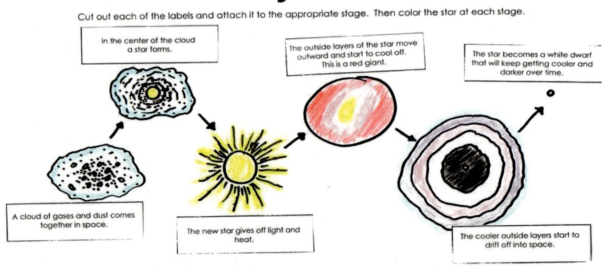

Ancient Egypt – Map Keys - Stars – Ancient Egyptian Art

😊 😊 **EXPLORATION: Mariner's Astrolabe**

Build a mariner's astrolabe to measure the height of a star. A mariner's astrolabe can be used to find your latitude on earth or to find the altitude of a star or the height of a tree or mountain.

Materials:

- scrap wood
- string
- 2 washers
- 1/4 x 1 inch hex bolt
- straw
- 2 straight pins
- paint
- protractor

1. Draw a circle with a twelve inch diameter on to a piece of scrap wood and cut it out with a jigsaw. Alternatively, you can use cardboard, but if you do, make sure to hang some washers from the bottom to act as weights so your astrolabe doesn't flap around in the breeze.
2. Poke a hole through the exact center of the circle. Enlarge the hole until a 1/4 x 1 inch hex bolt will fit through the hole.
3. Paint your astrolabe circle any way you like. Let it dry.
4. Use a ruler to draw a straight line through the center of the circle. Label both ends of the circle "0" degrees.
5. Set a protractor on the zero line and mark 30, 60, and 90 degrees in each quadrant. Label them.
6. Make a sighting arm by drilling a hole in the middle of a 10 x 1 x 1/2 inch piece of wood. The hole should be a little larger than the hex bolt. Paint the sighting arm in a contrasting color.
7. Assemble the astrolabe by putting a washer on a bolt, sliding the bolt through the hole of the wood, adding another washer, then putting the bolt through the dial. Finish with a wing nut on the bolt to keep it all together.

Additional Layer

The Zodiac is a group of 12 constellations that rotate through the sky from east to west in the same path that the sun travels. They were described by the ancient Greeks, who named most of them after animals—the root "zo" means animal. Today people speak of their sign, meaning the time of the year when a particular constellation of the zodiac was straight overhead when they were born.

On the Web

Celebrate the sun, our favorite star, by making this crayon sun catcher. Find the instructions at http://www.layers-of-learning.com/sun-catchers/

Ancient Egypt – Map Keys – Stars – Ancient Egyptian Art

Writer's Workshop

Learn the story of one of the constellations. Re-write it in your own words. Include illustrations.

Constellaiton Gemini

Additional Layer

Discuss how the pole star can be used to determine your latitude.

The pole star is almost exactly over the north pole of the earth, and so from our perspective it does not appear to move like the other stars.

Discuss why sailors had a much harder time determining longitude in the days before GPS and radio.

There is no constant star east or west. Sailors relied on charts and they kept careful track of their distance in a log book. Sometimes the charts weren't very good or non-existent and sometimes the distances recorded were not accurate.

8. Cut a straw to the same length as the sighting arm. Push the two pins through the straw and into the sighting arm about one inch from the ends, so that the sighting arm and the straw are parallel.
9. Put a hole at one 90 degree mark and tie a string through it to be a handle as you hold the astrolabe. If you used cardboard, you will need to put another hole opposite the first and hang washers from a string to add weight.

How to use your astrolabe:

Hold it by the loop from your outstretched arm so that the instrument hangs freely. To measure the altitude of a star, move the wooden sighting arm so that you can sight a star though the straw. The angle the sighting arm points to is the angle of the star above the horizon, or the altitude of the star.

To find your latitude on earth, measure the angle from the horizon to the pole star. Your latitude is equal to the angle between the horizon and the pole star.

To find the height of an object, such as a tree or a mountain, sight the top of the object, read the angle between the ground and the top of the object. Now you must measure the distance between yourself, or the place you took the angle reading from and the base of the object. If you are measuring the height of a mountain, you must use a map to find this distance. If you are measuring the height of a tree or building, you can measure the distance with a tape measure, either round to the nearest foot (or meter) or convert all measurements into smaller units (either inches or centimeters, whichever you prefer).

Now you know the angle and the adjacent side, or the distance. Imagine a triangle, with one angle at the base, one angle at the top of the object and one angle where you are standing. Let's say your angle is 45 degrees. Let's say the distance from the object to you is 50 feet. To find the height of the object, you multiply the tangent of the angle by 50 feet. Use a scientific calculator. Enter "tan" 45 x 50 = and you get 50, so the object is 50 feet tall.

Here's the formula: tan (angle) x (distance) = (height)

ANCIENT EGYPT – MAP KEYS - STARS – ANCIENT EGYPTIAN ART

😊 😊 EXPERIMENT: Star Map

Use your astrolabe to find the altitudes of some of the brighter stars and make a star map. Use graph paper and put a heavy line on each side for the east and west horizons. Draw a line through the center from east to west and one from north to south. Mark these lines 90°. Then mark the paper to show 15, 30, 45, 60, and 75 degrees from each side. Remember to plot the stars' distance from the north and south horizons as well as the east and west horizons. Straight up should be 90 degrees. Don't try to plot every star, just pick a couple of familiar constellations or the brightest stars in the sky. Put the date and time on your star map, because the sky changes every night. Do another star map a month later and plot the same stars. How much have they moved in a month?

Star chart written by Charles Messier, 1764

😊 😊 EXPLORATION: Light-Years Away

Because stars are so far away, we don't measure their distance in miles; we use light-years. A light-year is the distance light travels in one year, or about 6 trillion miles. Can you figure out how many miles away these stars are given their light-years? Get ready for some BIG numbers!

STAR	LIGHT-YEARS FROM EARTH	MILES FROM EARTH
Sirius	9 light-years	
Betelgeuse	500 light-years	
Rigel	800 light-years	
Deneb	1,600 light years	

Fabulous Fact

Astronomy is one of the only scientific fields left where an amateur can still make profound and essential discoveries which contribute to the scientific body of knowledge.

Famous Folks

Aristillus, a Greek who worked at the Library of Alexandria, created the first star catalog to keep track of and name stars observed in the night sky.

The upper Moon crater with the peak in the center is named after Aristillus. *Photo by NASA*

Fabulous Fact

The sun is a single star, but most stars in the universe are in pairs or triplets or larger groups, which revolve around a common center of gravity.

The Arts: Ancient Egyptian Art

Explanation

Memory work is good for kids and adults, whether it's a poem, the U.S. states, or the times tables. Exercising the brain will pay off later on when studying the nomenclature in zoology class, recalling potential clients from a business meeting, or staying up to date on the myriad of drugs that might help a patient's ailments.

Create a CD using your computer. You need a microphone. Most computers come with them and if yours doesn't have one, then you can pick one up for $10 or so. If your computer doesn't come with recording software, you can download Audacity, a simple and easy to use program, for free.

Look over the information you'll be covering in your studies for the next term or year and choose some info you'd like the kids to learn. Record it and play it back over and over as you memorize together.

Michelle

Ancient Egyptian art included paintings, sculpture, crafts, and architecture. A vast amount of Egyptian artwork that we still have today came from tombs and pyramids and emphasizes an afterlife.

Architects of the pyramids meticulously cut the stones so they would fit precisely together. They used ramps, much like the scaffolding of today's construction workers, to build the walls higher and higher. After the pyramid was completed, artisans decorated the structures with hieroglyphs and artwork. They also sculpted figures into the walls. The tombs were filled with sculptures, pottery, jewelry, and paintings, along with the mummies and the things they planned to take with them to the afterlife.

The Egyptian Book of the Dead was a particularly interesting piece of ancient artwork. It was a long scroll that was made of papyrus, a kind of paper made from a papyrus plant. It had instructions on it. These instructions taught the Egyptians how to get from this world to the afterlife. Ancient Egyptians weren't really afraid to die because they believed strongly that after they died they would go to the afterlife and live happily ever after (kind of like how many people now believe they will go to heaven when they die). The Egyptians believed the afterlife was just like Earth, except perfect because it was ruled by Osiris, the Egyptian God of the Dead. The Egyptian Book of the Dead was like a guidebook for navigating to a happy afterlife.

Ancient Egyptians valued artwork for its usefulness and its beauty. They used it to communicate their stories, myths, and ideas, and beautified their buildings with it. It was detailed and ornate, full of vibrant colors, and infused with symbolism.

☺ ☺ ☺ **EXPLORATION: Book of the Dead**
Choose a character (this could be a person, an animal, or anything else you want) that has just died and needs to get back

ANCIENT EGYPT – MAP KEYS - STARS – ANCIENT EGYPTIAN ART

to heaven. The Egyptian Book of the Dead showed the special things the dead person had to do— please the gods, navigate sacred rivers, and have his heart weighed. The person had to get through a series of obstacles, like an obstacle course, to make it to the afterlife. Think of at least 3 obstacles your character needs to overcome.

Now take a long piece of paper and divide it into 5 parts. In the first section, draw your character dead. In the next three frames, draw and write about the 3 obstacles they must overcome. In the final frame, show the character in heaven. Now roll it up and tie it with string or yarn so it looks like a scroll.

> **Additional Layer**
> Does it seem strange that people would go to so much work for dead people who can't even enjoy it? What do we do for our dead today?

Older kids may want to research the symbolism of this papyrus and find out what the Egyptians believed the dead had to do.

☺ ☺ ☺ EXPLORATION: Paper Making

The word "paper" comes from the word "papyrus." Papyrus was a plant used by the ancients to write on. Make your own paper from dryer lint, newspaper, or any other old papers and scraps you have lying around. Tear your papers into small pieces. Make sure to remove any staples, plastic, stickers, or any other impurities. Keep in mind that the lighter the paper you use, the lighter your paper will be. Darker paper or lots of ink will create a more gray and darker shade of paper. Rip the scraps up and put them in a blender until it's halfway full. Fill the blender with warm water and blend until the pulp is nice and smooth.

Now build a frame. Just stretch window screen material over an old picture frame. Pull the screen tight. The frame needs to be big enough to hold the paper you're making. Put the frame in a basin to catch the drippings, then pour the pulp you blended into your frame. You may want to stir in 2 teaspoons of liquid starch into your mixture if you're planning on writing on the paper; this helps ink from being absorbed into the paper later.

> **Additional Layer**
> The Egyptians used grid systems to help them keep the proportions correct for their figures. Learn how to draw a face proportionally using a grid system. Draw a long oval then divide the oval into three parts vertically and two horizontal parts. The eyes and nose go in the middle section and the mouth goes in the bottom section. The top section is all forehead and hairline. Look at someone's face and see if that is really how faces are proportioned. Where do the ears go?

Ancient Egypt – Map Keys – Stars – Ancient Egyptian Art

Adventure Story

Egyptians wrote and read many different types of literature from simple folk tales to how-to books. One famous tale we know of today is called *The Tale of the Shipwrecked Sailor*.

It tells of a young man who went abroad, but became shipwrecked and stranded in a foreign land. Like all Egyptians, his greatest fear is that he will die outside his beloved Egypt. The tale is full of adventure in the style of Sinbad the Sailor.

You can find the whole story at www.storynory.com.

Put a piece of felt over your pulp and use a wood block to press all the water out of the paper and through the screen, collecting in the basin. Then use washcloths to press even more water out. Once you've pressed all the water out that you can, gently lift the felt and see your new piece of paper. Very carefully remove it from the felt and set your paper out to dry.

🙂 🙂 🙂 **EXPEDITION: Virtual Egyptian Museum**

Although it would be amazing to actually go to Egypt, for most of us that's not possible. Instead of grabbing your passport, sit down in a comfy chair for this "armchair expedition." An armchair expedition is a virtual field trip that you can take in the comfort of your favorite chair in front of the television set or computer.

Go to the Virtual Egyptian Museum online at www.virtual-egyptian-museum.org for an amazing look at a lot of ancient Egyptian art.

EXPLANATION: Visuals

Learning about art history is best done when you can see a lot of examples of the art from the time period or artist. Get several art books or do a search on the internet for the unit you're studying. As kids look at lots of examples they can begin to identify the similarities and trends from the time. A simple question like, "What do these two paintings have in common?" can lead to a discussion about definitive characteristics of a time period. The profile faces of ancient Egyptian art, called frontalism, is one of these definitive characteristics.

Fabulous Fact

These are papyrus plants, from which the Egyptian paper was made. They grow on the banks of the Nile River and can get up to 15 feet tall. Besides using them to make papyrus paper, Egyptians also used them to make mattresses, chairs, and boats.

Ancient Egypt – Map Keys – Stars – Ancient Egyptian Art

😊 😊 😊 **EXPLORATION: Draw Like An Egyptian**
Draw a person in the style of Egyptian figures. Just follow these simple rules:

1. Always draw the head and neck from a side view. The lips and nose are from the side view too. Add one eye the way it would look from the front. Don't forget the one eyebrow.
2. Draw the shoulders and chest from the front.
3. The hips, legs, and feet should be drawn from the side. Usually men wore short skirts while women wore long, straight dresses.
4. Color it using vibrant colors and tanned skin as the Egyptians did.

It's perfectly fine to find an example of an Egyptian figure and copy it. Great artists always learn by copying the masters.

😊 😊 😊 **EXPLORATION: Canopic Jars**
As part of the embalming process, most of the organs of the dead person were removed and put aside into special jars, called canopic jars. The canopic jars became works of art as well.

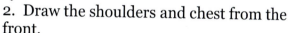

You can make a canopic jar. Save a used pump bottle from liquid soap or a container of similar size and shape. Cover it completely with paper maché, smooth it out, and allow to dry. Once it's dry you can gently sand the paper maché to make it smoother if you like.
Now paint it light brown. Once your paint is dry, write some hieroglyphic figures on the front with ink.

Additional Layer
There were rules for painters in ancient Egypt. Look at the angles of people in Egyptian paintings. See how their feet are facing sideways, but their chest is facing outward? One of their rules was to paint from the easiest angle to recognize. What do you notice about their faces? Their eyes?

This style is called frontalism.

Music
Some popular Egyptian instruments included the harp, the flute, the ney and the oud.

Here is a woman playing a ney.

Additional Layer
We have found a lot of ancient art in the tombs of kings and pharaohs. Why do you think they kept art in their tombs? Go find out why.

Ancient Egypt – Map Keys – Stars – Ancient Egyptian Art

Additional Layer
What do you believe about death and what happens after we die? Why do you think so much art is focused on this theme?

Angel Musician by Melozzo da Forli, circa 1480

Additional Layer

In a way, Egyptian artists who worked in teams were more like our modern-day interior designers than our artists. They were hired to work together to decorate the walls and artifacts of the community.

Additional Layer
The Egyptians weren't the only ones who painted their tombs; check out the Etruscans, the Chinese, and the Koreans.

Next comes the lid. Egyptians shaped the lids of the jars to look like animals heads, usually to represent one of the gods who often had a part human, part animal body. There might be a falcon or a lion or a hippo. Pick an animal you like and shape a lid out of clay to look like the animal head. Place the clay over the neck of the jar to be sure it will fit. Bake or allow the clay to dry according to the directions on the package. Paint the head shaped lid any way you like.

☺ ☺ ☻ EXPEDITION: Time Warp Art
Visit http://www.egyptiartsite.com/warp.html for an armchair expedition. This site is interesting because it is the work of a modern artist who enjoys creating in the style of ancient Egyptians. You can identify modern themes within the style of the ancients.

☺ ☺ ☻ EXPLORATION: Team Effort
Most artists today work alone. They decide what they want to create and make their piece independently. In ancient Egypt, this was not so. They worked in teams to decorate murals and create the art that was one of the hallmarks of their entire civilization.

A supervisor would sketch a plan first. Some artisans were assigned to plaster the walls, some to sketch the design, and others to fill in the colors and details. Meanwhile, the supervisor was the overseer and constantly checked to make sure the artists were doing everything right.

You can try this too. Get in teams and decide on a supervisor. The supervisor will sketch a small scale drawing using crayons or colored pencils. Hang a piece of butcher paper or poster board on the wall. Someone will sketch the design based on the small-scale drawing. Someone else will do the black ink outlines. Still others will be responsible for painting in the colors and details.

☺ ☺ EXPLORATION: Sarcophagus
Using the sarcophagus outline drawing at the end of this unit, create your own sarcophagus. Decorate it with things that represent you. You can cut out the front and back and glue it to a cut-to-size paper towel roll for a more 3-D look.

Ancient Egypt – Map Keys - Stars – Ancient Egyptian Art

🙂 🟢 EXPLORATION: Black Cats

A mummified cat

Both Upper and Lower Egypt had religious beliefs that included the worship of animals, including cats. Cats represented grace and poise. One Egyptian goddess, Bastet, was in the form of a cat. Some cats were even mummified like people because of their importance. As you learn about the place of honor cats held for the Egyptians, make this cat mask. Use the printable from this unit to trace your design on to paper. Then decorate your cat mask. We used black construction paper, a small piece of pink felt behind the nose, and glitter. For older kids, *The Cat of Bubastes* by G.A. Henty is a really great read about a young Egyptian who accidentally kills a sacred cat.

EXPLANATION: Columns

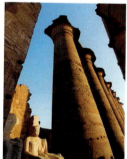

We often think of the ancient Greeks when we see columns in architecture. Actually, the first columns we know of were Egyptian. The pyramids, temples, and buildings of Egypt have many stone columns. We think that the first built were the 40 columns at the palace of King Zoser. It's likely that the Greeks got the idea of columns from the Egyptians.

Famous Folks

Imhotep was the architect who built King Zoser's pyramid. He was also a scribe, physician, philosopher, and the royal vizier, and revered as a god.

Additional Layer

The pyramids themselves were great works of art. The largest is the great pyramid at Khufu. Each of its sandstone blocks weigh about two and a half tons - more than a car!

Coming up next . . .

Unit 1-3
Ancient Europe
Global Grids
Earth & Moon - Crafts

Ancient Egypt – Map Keys - Stars – Ancient Egyptian Art

My Ideas For This Unit:

Title: _____ Topic: _____

_____
_____
_____
_____
_____
_____
_____
_____
_____

Title: _____ Topic: _____

_____
_____
_____
_____
_____
_____
_____
_____
_____

Title: _____ Topic: _____

_____
_____
_____
_____
_____
_____
_____
_____
_____

Ancient Egypt – Map Keys - Stars – Ancient Egyptian Art

My Ideas For This Unit:

Title: _____ Topic: _____

_____
_____
_____
_____
_____
_____
_____
_____
_____

Title: _____ Topic: _____

_____
_____
_____
_____
_____
_____
_____
_____
_____
_____

Title: _____ Topic: _____

_____
_____
_____
_____
_____
_____
_____
_____
_____

King Tutankhamen

This is King Tut's death mask. King Tut is famous not because he was the greatest of the Egyptian pharaohs, but because he was so young – only 18 when he died. His tomb was discovered in 1922 by a man named Howard Carter. It was quite a find because most of the tombs had already been discovered and raided by that time.

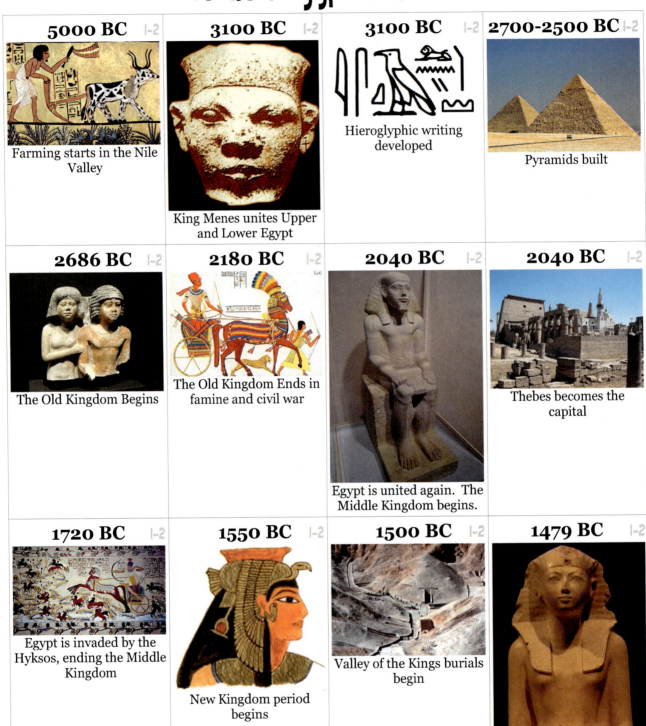

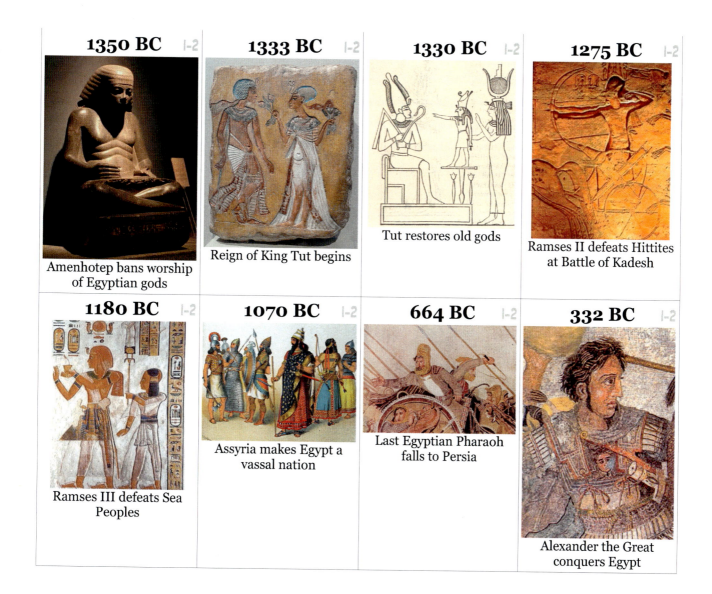

City Map

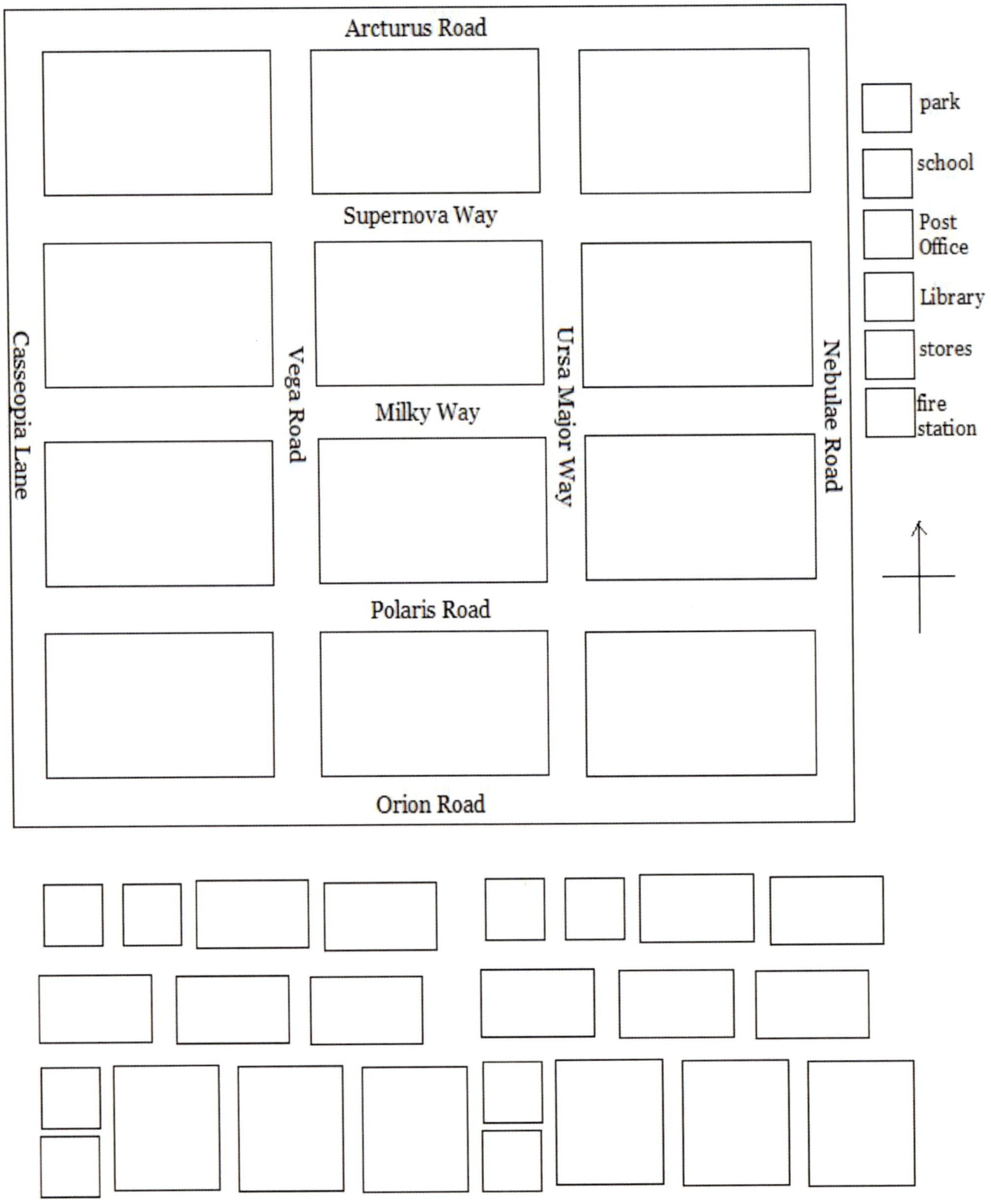

Arcturus Road
Supernova Way
Milky Way
Polaris Road
Orion Road

Casseopia Lane
Vega Road
Ursa Major Way
Nebulae Road

- park
- school
- Post Office
- Library
- stores
- fire station

Layers of Learning

The Life Cycle of A Star

Cut out each of the labels and attach it to the appropriate stage. Then color the star at each stage.

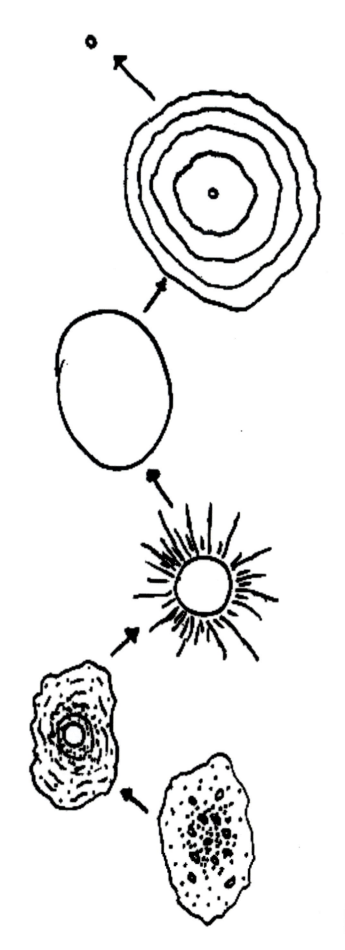

A cloud of gases and dust comes together in space.	The new star gives off light and heat.	The cooler outside layers start to drift off into space.
In the center of the cloud a star forms.	The outside layers of the star move outward and start to cool off. This is a red giant.	The star becomes a white dwarf that will keep getting cooler and darker over time.

Layers of Learning

_____ Island Treasure Map

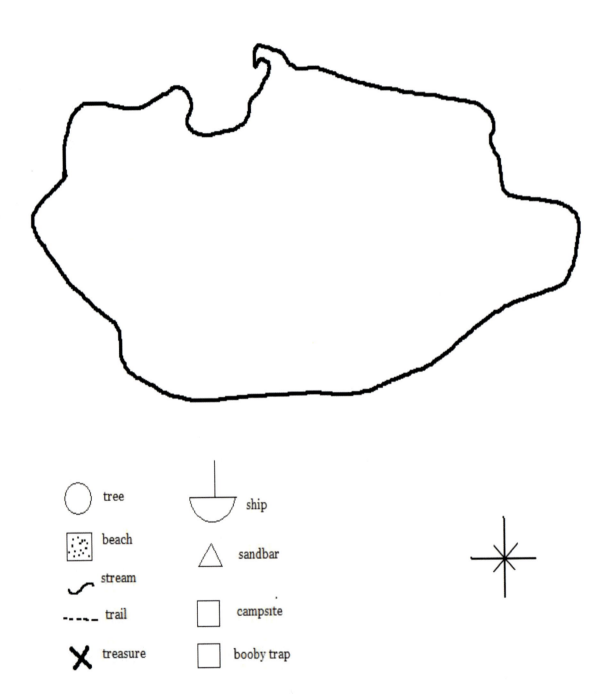

Decorate Your Own Sarcophagus

If you want to be authentic, you may want to include:
- false eyes so the mummy can look out
- a door so the mummy's spirit can come and go
- a scarab beetle for luck
- jewelry to show how rich and important you are

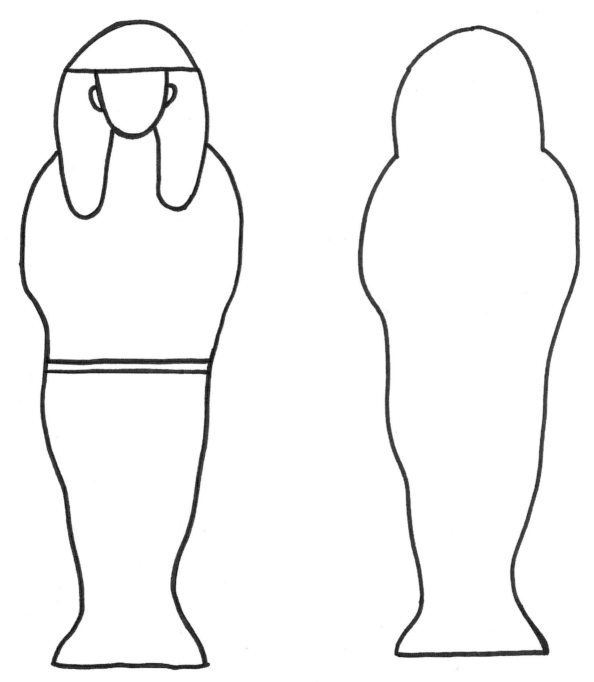

Egyptian Cat Mask

Layers of Learning

ABOUT THE AUTHORS

Karen & Michelle . . .
Mothers, sisters, teachers, women who are passionate
about educating kids.
We are dedicated to lifelong learning.

Karen, a mother of four, who has homeschooled her kids for more than eight years with her husband, Bob, has a bachelor's degree in child development with an emphasis in education. She lives in Utah where she gardens, teaches piano, and plays an excruciating number of board games with her kids. Karen is our resident Arts expert and English guru {most necessary as Michelle regularly and carelessly mangles the English language and occasionally steps over the bounds of polite society}.

Michelle and her husband, Cameron, homeschooling now for over a decade, teach their six boys on their ten acres in beautiful Idaho country. Michelle earned a bachelors in biology, making her the resident Science expert, though she is mocked by her friends for being the *Botanist with the Black Thumb of Death*. She also is the go-to for History and Government. She believes in staying up late, hot chocolate, and a no whining policy. We both pitch in on Geography, in case you were wondering, and are on a continual quest for knowledge.

*Visit our constantly updated blog for tons of free ideas,
free printables, and more cool stuff for sale:*
www.Layers-of-Learning.com

Made in the USA
Columbia, SC
27 August 2020